MY PIGGY BANK OF POEMS

Yohaan Remedios

ISBN 978-93-5610-266-8

Published in India 2022 by Pencil

A brand of
One Point Six Technologies Pvt. Ltd.
123, Building J2, Shram Seva Premises,
Wadala Truck Terminal, Wadala (E)
Mumbai 400037, Maharashtra, INDIA
E connect@thepencilapp.com
W www.thepencilapp.com

Author biography

Yohaan Remedios is a budding sportsman, a good story reader and a lovely kid. He loves to try out new things. So he has come up with a beautiful book of poems called … MY PIGGY BANK OF POEMS!

CONTENTS

OUR POWER OUR ENERGY

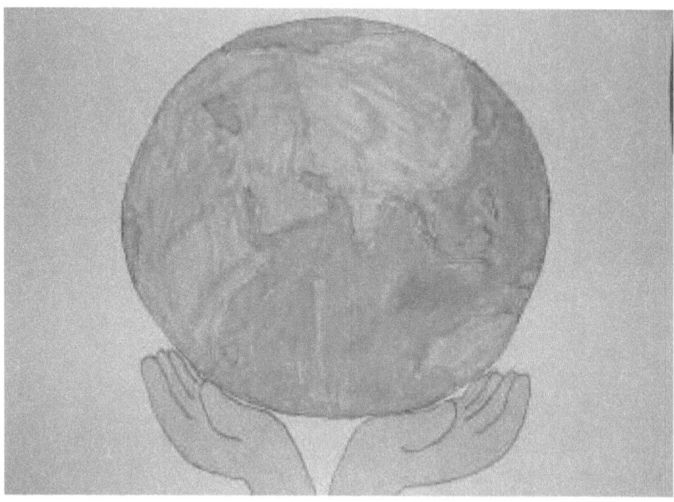

Our freedom fighters give us knowledge,
We will get energy to fight the British if we eat porridge.
Give us the power! Give us the power!
We keep ourself clean by having bath with the shower.
We get power by eating healthy food,
You will be strong,active and good.
You will get power if you do exercise.
You will have strong powerful eyes.

GOD IS MY LOVE

We are many people
I like to go to the temple.
Chatter chatter chatter, we solve the matter.
Your mouth will not be quite
Till I sleep through out the night.
God is my love we pray to lord.
My God, my Lord may we always do good.
God is a greenish tree
God is a lovely piece of me.
I love my puppy, I love my dove.

My God,My Lord you make me all of goodness.
God is giving so much love to me.
God's soul is the curve of life.
God has sparkly eyes to see,
Showing the vision of the sparkly eyes to me.
Showing the beauty of birds, animals and flies,
God never lies!

HEART

The trees are dancing
The geese are enjoying.
The heart is beating
The horse cart is fleeting.
Hearts are made of blood
The Yamuna river is like a flood.
To a mother, child is like flower bud
The plants are growing in the mud.
The flowers are shining in the sun
O my heart is having fun!
Gratify your heart…
O always Gratify your Heart!

MY CYCLE

My cycle,my friend
You have to drive till the end.
Among yourself among myself,
If you want to ride a cycle then have sense.
When can this cycle ,I drive?
I will give it to you at five.
Where is my bag? I am finding finding finding.
I went back home riding riding riding.

MY PARENTS

My mother is very nice.
She is good at catching mice.
My father went to Goa
And he likes to eat samosa.
Talk talk talk talk on the phone
And walk walk walk without taking us in the zone.
Pay pay money
And give me one spoon of honey.
Fighting with her husband
And lightning is suspend.
My mother reads books
And loves Florian Fuchs

PLAY

Play football but be very careful
Play some easy game like handball.
Play hockey but nicely,
Don't play like a donkey.
Play hard shots in the game of cricket
Be smart or you'll give away a wicket.
Play boxing but gently box
And don't get angry like an ox.

Play play play
Play every single day.

MOTHER POT

My mother is very nice
She is good at being wise.
She works and works in the night
The three boys let her have some light.
She goes to the ground
What luck a crazy husband found.
Dust always around
Seeing the phone the eyes became round.
My mother's cheeks are lovely pink
The three boys clean the sink.
My mother does work
She does exercise the first time then she
Gets a jerk.

LIFE

The winds are blowing,
The birds are flying
Beauty, beauty, beauty
The animals do their duty.
Elephants have a trunk
But they don't eat junk!
The flowers are yellow
In the sunshine they glow.
The clouds move
The garbage should be removed.

The trees are green
The garden is clean.
Green world !
Clean world!

GADGET

Fallen around all the phones
We have much money to have loans.
All the Apps around
Poor Earth has a dirty surround.
Broken Mind Broken Mind!
Seeing the phone our eyes become blind
Phone phone phone
Phone around the Home.
Phone is not important

Zone is Important
Seeing the laptop
Your mind will be flop.

FLOWING LEAVES

Flowing leaves in the water waves
The sunshine reflects on the caves
A beautiful flash on the world
God has made each one a lovely gold
The greenish mountain
A beautiful drip of rain.
A lovely water flow
God has made the sun to glow.
The blowing winds

The birds have little twins.
The lovely beautiful flowers
The lovely rain drop showers.

COLOUR

An apple is red.

I eat food and then I go
to sleep on the bed.

The ball is round and blue

The lovely birds flew.
The colour of the eggplant is purple
A creature walks very slow is a turtle.
The colour of her dress is pink
God has made the beautiful eyes to blink.
The beautiful leaves
An angry person screams.
My tshirt colour is black
I payed my friend 1 lakh.
Yellow Yellow Yellow Awesome fellow.
The light bulb colour is white
Yesterday I flew a kite.
The colour of the wall is grey
At the market every customer has to google pay.

MIRACLE

What a lovely beautiful glory
God I did mistakes then I am sorry.
In my life I have come up in progress
I don't think that I get much or less.
In the whole world there is much crowd
Don't put the volume so loud.
Many people have cheeks that are pink
Some animals are also extinct.

The sun is a golden round
In the sky like a diamond found.
A loving miracle hug
Beautiful insects like lady bug.

SMOOTHLY

I use a pen for smooth handwriting
Yesterday I wore a beautiful smooth ring.
Smooth Smooth Smooth everything goes
smoothly.

I am in a mood to write
for a pen or a pencil never fight.
Focus on writing focus on writing if you
write smoothly then good will be your handwriting.

The waving smooth water,
enjoy the smooth windy weather.

THE BODY

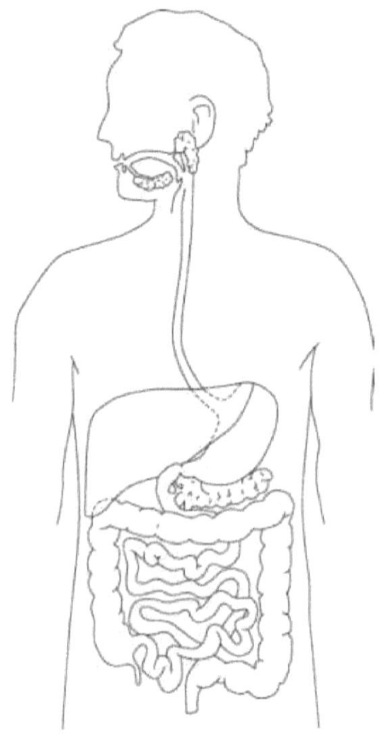

The rocket goes like a bullet
In the throat there is a gullet.
From illness protects our immunity,

The doctor does his own duty.
We all have two legs, for the body its good
To eat eggs.

The skin is light and lovely,
Everyone blinks their eyes slowly.
The eyes are very dark, after we are born
We get a birth mark.
We all have different types of hair,
If a person is injured then we should
Care.

To smell beautiful flowers we have a
Nose,

To be safe from corona virus we
Should take vaccine of first and second
Dose.

We all have our chest,
To be calm we should take rest.
We all have two hands,
God has given this life to go to new places
Like Australia, Goa or Netherlands.
Everyone have big big nails
If you don't do your studies then that child
fails.

BLUE SKY

Look up in the blue sky,
God has given the blue sky to show truth
not lie.
Look up in the blue sky,

The lovely blue sky, such a life is of mine.
Look up in the blue sky,
See God's love, God is sky blue dove.
What happened poor blue sky,
They are bursting crackers, but Why?
What happened poor blue sky,
If everyone burst fire crackers then
I will die.
Look up in the blue sky,
Today is first July.
Look up in the blue sky,
They are bursting crackers then I will
cry.
Look up in the blue sky,
I counted some birds, how many?
Five.
Look up in the blue sky,
See the comets whizzing by.

CHRISTMAS

Santa Claus gives gifts
the places are cleaned while Christmas
time like staircase, malls and lifts.
There are Santa caps, In the night we get

good sleeping naps. Yesterday Santa Claus
gave me a pen, Santa Claus lives in North Pole
not in a shop, building or a den.
Christmas Day is on the twenty fifth,
I will give him a car named Swift.
On twenty fifth of December Jesus was born,
Santa Claus can come in the evening
or morn.
Santa Claus give gifts to children like
a pen, doll or a book, Christmas Day is like
a fresh look.
Merry Christmas and a Happy New Year,
Santa Claus lives in North Pole , North Pole
is very far not near.
There are many decorations,
And Christmas celebrations.
Merry Christmas!!!

www.ingramcontent.com/pod-product-compliance
Lightning Source LLC
LaVergne TN
LVHW050429160726
843469LV00041B/1288

* 9 7 8 9 3 5 6 1 0 2 6 6 8 *